P9-DBT-953

AT HOME

© Aladdin Books Ltd 1989

Designed and produced by
Aladdin Books Ltd, 70 Old Compton Street, London
W1V 5PA, United Kingdom

Design: David West
        Children's Book Design

Illustrators: Tizzie Knowles, Louise Nevitt, Rob Shone
and Shaun Barlow

Pete Sanders is the head teacher of a North London
elementary school, and is working with teachers on
personal, social, and health education.

The publishers would like to thank Seamus, Kimber, Fiona,
Zara, Dominic, Bonny, Leila, Aminata, Miguel, James,
Alexandra, and all the other children who posed for the
pictures used in this book.

Published in the United States in 1989 by
Gloucester Press, 387 Park Avenue South, New York, NY 10016

ISBN 0 531 17148 5

Library of Congress Catalog
Card Number: 88-83108

Printed in Belgium

AT HOME

PETE SANDERS

GLOUCESTER PRESS
New York · London · Toronto · Sydney

Introduction

Are you safe at home? The outer walls of a house protect you from the cold and the rain. But inside there are lots of things that may be dangerous. People have to make sure their houses are as safe as possible.

To do this, we have to think about what situations can be dangerous and how to avoid them. This book shows you what kind of things to look out for.

Look at the house on this page. As in many people's houses there are a lot of things happening. Everyone is so busy that they're not being careful about safety. See how many danger points you can spot by looking very carefully at the picture. You'll find the answers on page 29.

Safety ideas

People have designed equipment to make houses safer. To protect you from burns there are firescreens that enclose fireplaces. Some children have pajamas made out of fireproof material. Kitchens have cupboards, so that cleaning powders and liquids that can make you sick are kept safely out of the way.

But it's not enough just to have safety equipment in your home, you have to use things in the right way. That is why people have safety routines, for example, switching lights off at night. At home you are probably told to put toys and clothes where they belong. You need to learn all these routines from other people. Many accidents happen because people are tired and forget about safety.

PROJECT

It's a good idea to think about routines that help to keep you safe. You can get so used to doing something that you do it without thinking and get it wrong. Try and work out your own night routine. On a piece of paper, write down all the things you should do before going to bed. Make sure the list is in the order that you should do them. Put it on your bedroom door.

NIGHT-TIME CHECKLIST:

1. Put toys away
2. Put slippers beside bed
3. Close window
4. Close door
5. Switch off lights

There are many dangers in kitchens. It's a particularly important place to keep safe.

In homes with fires like this, a guard can prevent accidents.

Things that can cut

Have you ever been cut by anything? Sharp objects can make you bleed. It's easy to hurt yourself with an opened can. That's why things like can lids should be thrown into a garbage can at once. Other sharp items have to be stored and used with care.

When you use scissors, it is best to cut away from yourself because they might slip and cut you. Even passing a knife needs to be thought about. Do you always remember to offer the handle of a knife for the other person to take?

We all break things from time to time. If you do have to clean up, it's important to use a dustpan and brush. Some bits may be so small it's hard to see them. Then you can mop up any liquid. If you break a plastic toy, throw it out.

INFORMATION

If you cut yourself, it's important to look after the wound. With a small cut you should stop the bleeding by placing it under running water from a tap. Then put a piece of clean cloth over it and hold it firmly. Clean the area around the cut and put a bandage on to stop dirt getting into it. Even though it may hurt a lot, it won't take a long time to heal.

A cut bleeds at first. Then the blood clots.

When the scab falls off, a new layer of skin can be seen.

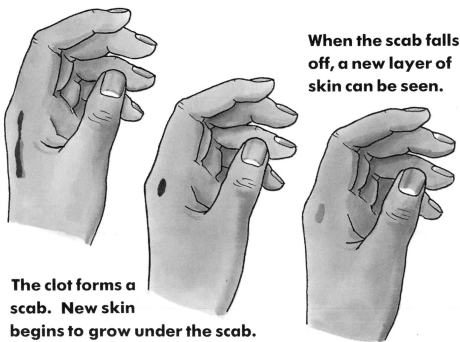

The clot forms a scab. New skin begins to grow under the scab.

There is a safe way of doing everything — even opening a can.

- Make a list of all the objects that are used for cutting and what they cut.

- Take some cardboard and cut it into rectangles.

- Draw cutting tools on half of the cards. On the other half draw things that can be cut.

- Play spit. When you or your friend get a pair shout "spit."

Things that hurt skin

It's not only cutting tools that can hurt the skin. Some of the objects on the left could hurt you if they were on the floor. That's why you should wear something on your feet at home. If you drop something sharp on the floor, it's important to try to find it. You could prevent an accident.

Tools can hurt you, so you have to be very careful with them. First, get an adult to show you how to use a tool. You need lots of practice to use a hammer without hurting yourself.

Insects like wasps and bees can hurt you with their sting. They may do this when they feel that they are going to be attacked. It's usually best to stay very still when there is a bee or wasp around and wait for it to fly away.

INFORMATION

The skin is a barrier that protects the inside of our bodies. It has two main layers. The outer one is the part that is waterproof. The inner layer has tiny pits to allow hair to grow. It also has blood vessels which nourish the skin, sweat glands and nerve endings. A bruise is a sign that you are bleeding underneath the skin.

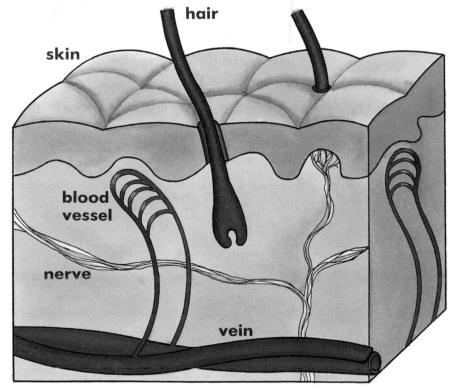

hair

skin

blood vessel

nerve

vein

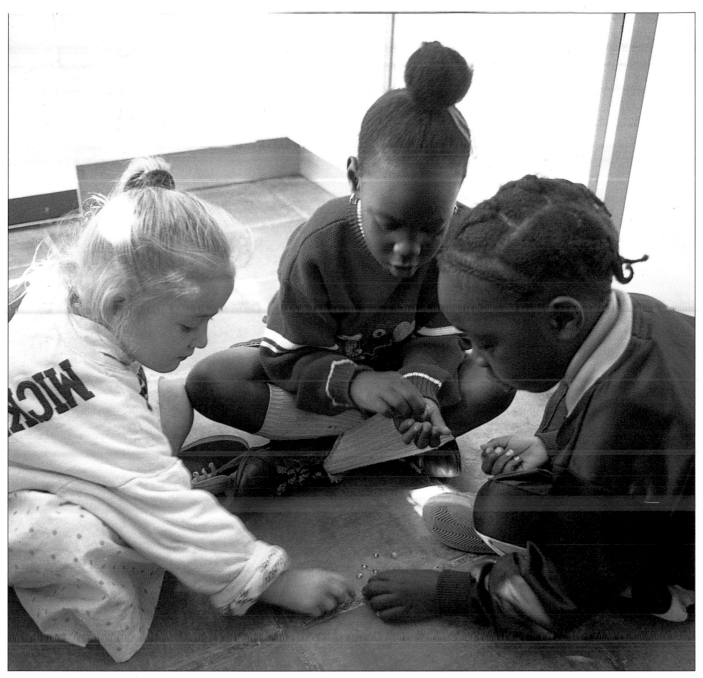

These girls are picking up thumb tacks. They know it has to be done carefully.

It's a good idea to wear shoes at home. You wear different kinds of shoes for different occasions. Most of us have ordinary everyday shoes, slippers and maybe some sports maybe some sneakers. Make up some silly pictures showing people wearing the wrong shoes for the activity they are doing. Draw them or else cut out pictures from magazines.

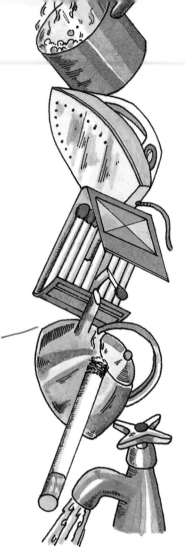

Things that can burn

Most people know that they shouldn't play with matches or cigarettes but fires aren't the only things that can burn you. There are many appliances – like irons and the oven – that can do this. Electric blankets can start fires. It's not a good idea to put toys or clothes on radiators. It's important to switch off machines when they are not in use.

Scalds are burns caused by wet heat, like showers that are too hot. Before you get into the bathtub, make sure that the water is not too hot. Knocking saucepans over in the kitchen can cause scalds. Steam from a kettle or from any very hot liquids can be a problem too. If you are passing someone a hot drink, you have to do it very carefully.

 **PROJECT**

Ask an adult to help you with this experiment. You can make a simple fire extinguisher. Be sure the candle is firmly stuck to the saucer. Put one tablespoon full of baking soda and two teaspoons of vinegar into a glass. This will make bubbles of carbon dioxide. Take a tube, and tip the mixture down it. The flame will go out because carbon dioxide doesn't burn.

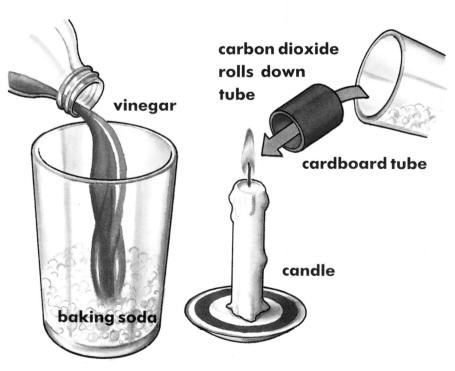

vinegar

baking soda

carbon dioxide rolls down tube

cardboard tube

candle

Adults do not always think of safety. They may forget hot drinks can scald.

Hot water from a tap in the bathroom can scald you.

Electricity

Electricity travels along wires and reaches the outlets in our homes. Plugs go in the outlets and connect machines with electricity. Electric wires are usually covered by material which electricity doesn't travel through, like glass or rubber. This type of material is called insulation. It's safe to hold an electric wire as long as it is fully covered.

Touching a bare wire can give you an electric shock. Playing with an outlet or with electric tools is very risky. Electricity can travel through water so you shouldn't use electric appliances in the bathroom. It is also important to make sure that you have dry hands, dry feet, and are wearing shoes whenever you plug something in.

PROJECT

Ask an adult to help you with this experiment. This experiment shows how well electricity travels through water. You need three pieces of wire, a battery, a bulb in an outlet and a container. Set up the experiment as shown in the diagram. Put the water in last. Do not put your hands in the water. Switch the experiment off by taking a wire off the battery.

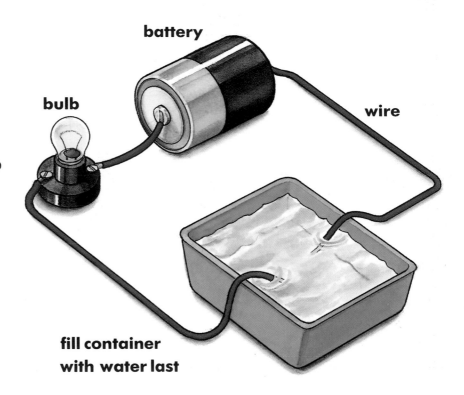

battery

bulb

wire

fill container
with water last

When you help with housework, make sure no one can trip over a hanging cord.

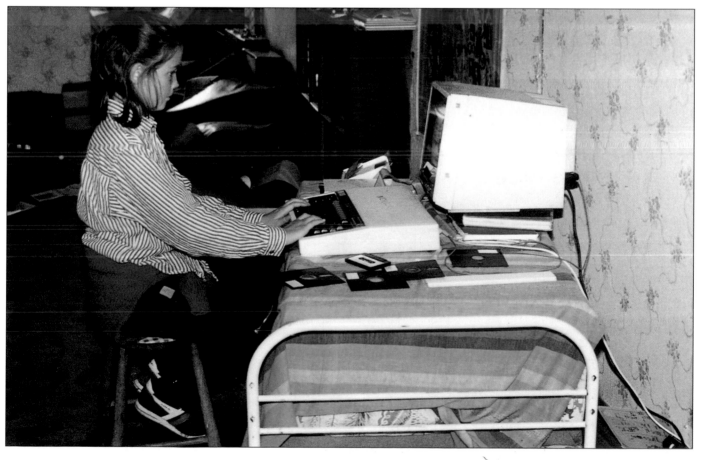

Electric cords should never be left trailing on the ground.

Poisoning and choking

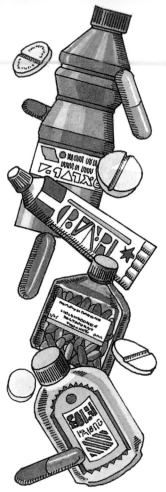

It's not just cleaning liquids and powders that can make you sick. Medicines can too. The labels on medicines tell us the amount to take because having too much can harm us. Some medicines taste good but they're not for drinking or eating.

You may choke if you eat too fast so it's a good idea to chew food really well before swallowing it. Babies don't know this and have to learn. Peanuts are dangerous for them because they can get stuck inside their throats.

Germs can make you ill. That is why you have to be careful to keep things clean. Spoiled food should never be eaten.

INFORMATION

Water that we've used (from sinks, baths, showers and toilets) can cause disease. When water leaves your house through pipes, it goes through bigger pipes to a sewage treatment plant. There the water is cleaned by going through screens, grit chambers and tanks. Once this has been done, the water goes back into lakes and rivers, and starts its journey to our homes again.

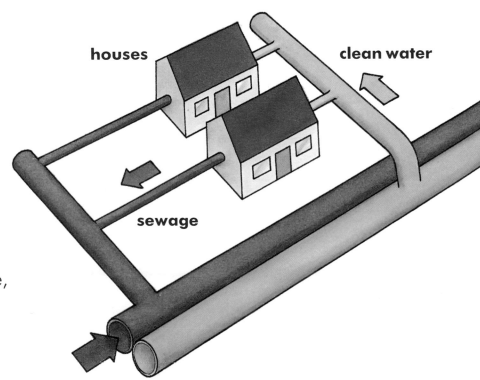

houses

clean water

sewage

If you need to take medicine, ask an adult to make sure you take the right dose.

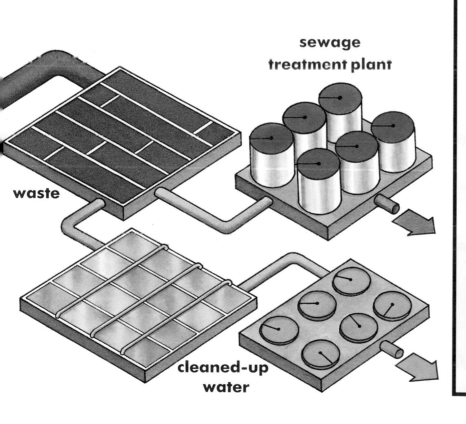

sewage
treatment plant

waste

cleaned-up
water

● Jingles are songs that advertise products on television and radio.

● Make up your own jingle to help keep people safe. It might be using a poem or a song. You may even want to write your own tune.

● Try to remind people not to do anything that might make them sick.

Falling down

Think of the last time you fell down and why you fell. It may have happened because you were trying to do things too quickly or perhaps you were tired. Maybe someone left something lying around and you stumbled over it. It's easy to trip if you're not wearing the right shoes.

Rugs and mats can make you fall down. Some people have non-slip bathroom mats which stick to the floor. Wet floors can be very slippery. That's why it is wise to mop up anything you spill as soon as possible.

Many children enjoy jumping and playing on stairs, without thinking about the risks of falling down. It's not a good idea to play on the stairs, especially if there are toddlers around. They can be unsteady on the stairs.

 PROJECT

Lots of people find it very boring to clean up after doing something. But if things were kept in their proper places, then there wouldn't be so many accidents in the home. How many differences can you spot between these two pictures? What kind of things would an adult leave lying around that could be dangerous? Make a list of all the things you can think of.

Although it may seem fun, playing on the stairs causes many accidents.

Safety gates prevent accidents.

Breathing

Breathing air gets oxygen into our lungs. It goes into our bloodstream and gives us energy and warmth. Breathing is something you don't have to remember to do.

It is possible to drown in just a few inches of water, because it stops air from reaching your lungs. When playing in the bath or a wading pool, take care and look out for your friends.

Plastic bags also stop air from getting into your lungs. Some babies and children have killed themselves by putting a plastic bag over their heads.

Flames from fires are very dangerous but it is often the fumes from the smoke that stop people from getting enough oxygen. Closed doors stop smoke from spreading.

PROJECT

We take air for granted. But try this experiment. Put a jar over a candle on a saucer. How long does it take the candle to go out? The flame goes out because the jar cuts off the supply of air. Things need air to burn so the easiest way to put out a fire is to cut off the air. You can time how long it takes for the candle to go out. Try the experiment with jars of different sizes.

candle

saucer

Get an adult to help you with this experiment.

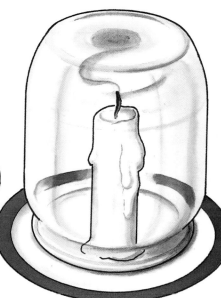

after a short while the candle goes out

If plastic bags are left lying around, young children might hurt themselves.

MIND THE STEP

Posters are used to present information so we take notice. They don't usually have many words on them. Think of different safety messages for each room in your house.

Which room needs the most safety messages? Design a poster for that room which shows all the information you have collected. Use bold letters and think of a catchy title.

In the yard

Being in a yard or playground is great fun. You can run around and play exciting games. The trouble is you can get careless. If you've ever aimed a ball badly, you probably know about the dangers of broken glass.

There are many small sharp objects that you can't see in the soil or grass. Wearing shoes is important. If you've had splinters, you know how annoying they are. That's why you have to be careful with things made out of wood.

Adults use many different tools for gardening. There are rakes, spades, lawnmowers and many others. If they're not used properly they can cause accidents. Rakes shouldn't be left lying around because if you step on them they could hurt you.

INFORMATION

Some children have poisoned themselves by chewing plants. Here are some of the plants that can hurt you. Nettles can sting you. Thorns can scratch you. Many red berries are poisonous and shouldn't be eaten. Another problem is that adults use chemicals to kill weeds and pests and help the grass and flowers grow. These are very dangerous.

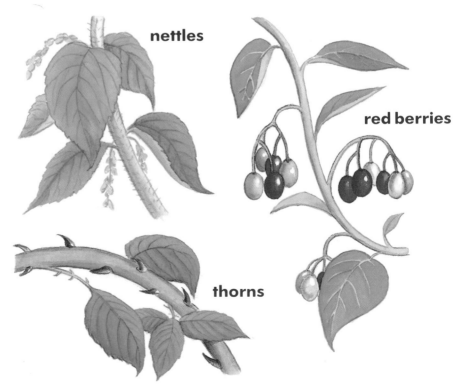

nettles

red berries

thorns

Remembering to play safe games is hard, especially when you get excited.

Some children use adult tools as toys. They don't realize that this is risky.

Thinking about others

Others may not be able to look after themselves as well as you. Think about the people who live in your neighborhood. Probably there are elderly people who need help. Can you think why this should be so?

Toddlers need to be helped because they don't know as much as you do. They might want to play with the knobs on the stove. Little fingers can go into electric outlets.

People with disabilities may need special equipment to help keep them safe. Many of these things would make all homes safer. Wider doorways would be helpful for everyone as well as for people in wheelchairs.

PROJECT

Think of someone who has special needs. Plan a room which would help that person keep safe. For example, you may want to attach flashing lights to the telephone so that someone who can't hear very well can answer it. A blind person would need special cooking utensils. Before you begin your plan think about the size that you need to make objects for easy use. What colors will you use?

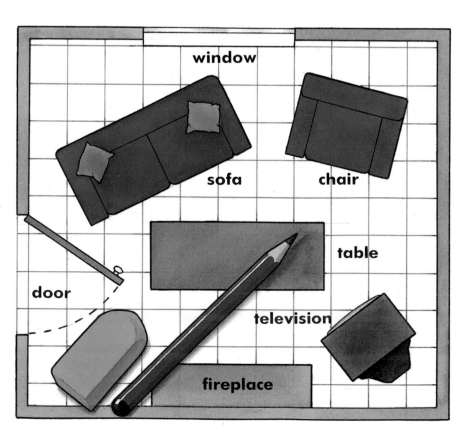

You can help younger children learn about staying safe.

Toddlers may enjoy tugging a tablecloth – with disastrous results.

Keeping safe

Being safe at home means putting what you know into action. Think before taking risks. One of the simplest ways of staying safe is knowing where things belong and making sure that they are put away. Even remembering not to slam doors can help – you might trap your own or someone else's fingers.

You probably know what to do if you cut yourself. It's always a good idea to talk to an adult if you have had an accident of any kind. For example, a cut may need further treatment from a doctor. It's very easy to panic if you have an accident. Although staying calm is hard, you must try to do this so you can think more clearly about what to do. A cool head in a crisis can spare you and others a lot of pain and suffering.

INFORMATION

It is quite common for cooking oil to catch fire in a saucepan or frying pan. Putting water onto the flames will not put the fire out. This is what to do if there is no adult available: Turn off the stove (1). Take a towel and put it under the tap (2). Squeeze out the towel. Place it over the pan (3). This cuts off the air supply and puts out the fire.

26

Washing an apple gets rid of the chemicals and dirt on its skin.

3

Rough games can get out of hand.

Safety game

Most accidents in the home happen because people forget to do things, or because they are tired. Perhaps they haven't learned about safety in the first place.

Now that you know more about home safety, you can help other people by sharing your ideas. You may have thought of different ways of doing this already. It may be that they don't know as much as you do! Try them out on your friends and have fun!

PROJECT

You may want to try a safety and hazard game. There is one printed for you to copy here. You will need a die and a counter for each player. Write in the rules where they go, for example, go back five spaces when you spill a drink. You could make up your own game.

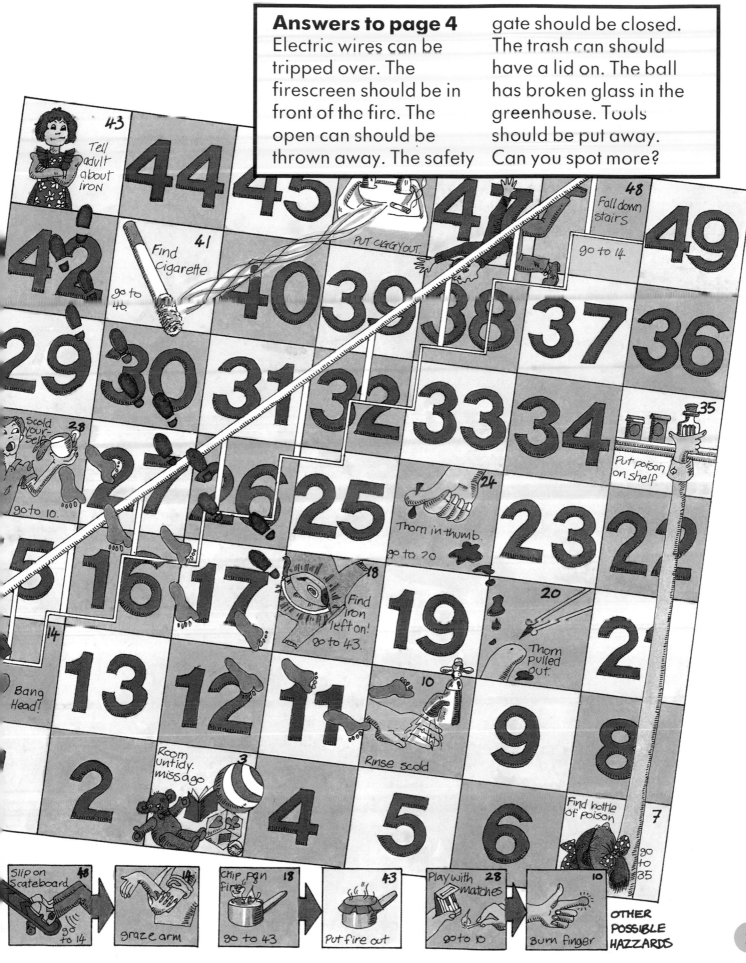

First Aid

First aid is giving care and help to someone who is hurt. It is important to stay calm, so that everyone can think clearly, and put the person at ease. Also, if you give first aid to someone, you will need to tell an adult what you have done. It's very important to get help as soon as possible. This might be from any adult or from a medical expert.

What to do with burns

They can be caused by dry or wet heat, by electricity or chemicals. Don't put any lotions onto the burn, or try to remove any loose skin. Cool the burn by running the injured part of the body under the cold water tap for up to 30 minutes but don't use ice. Dry the burned area and cover it with a clean non-fluffy dressing such as a handkerchief or a sheet. Don't use cotton because this may stick to the skin.

Cuts and bruises

If someone has a bruise, raise that part of the body to make the person more comfortable. If you do not have an ice pack, run a clean cloth under a tap and squeeze it out. Use this to press just below where the bruise is. This will help to stop the bleeding underneath the skin and reduce the bruising and swelling.

If someone has a cut that is still bleeding, place a clean pad over it and press the pad to stop the flow of blood. You must make sure that dirt doesn't go into the cut. Wipe away any dirt, and cover the cut with a clean piece of material. Remember to clean **away** from the wound. Again, do not use cotton, as this may get into the cut.

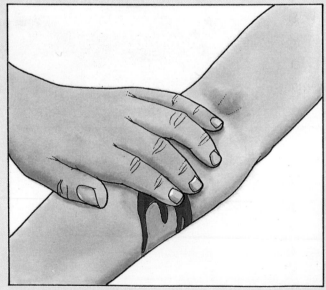

Abrasions (scrapes) should be treated in the same way. They often contain dirt or grit, which can get stuck and cause infections. Make sure that you remove all the dirt from the site. Then put a clean piece of material on the abrasion.

Sprains

They usually happen to wrists and ankles. If someone has a sprain, help them to get into a comfortable position. Raise the part of the body where the sprain is. Take an ice pack or a cloth that has been put under a cold water tap and squeezed out. Wrap this around the sprained area. This should be done for at least 30

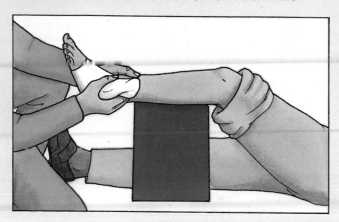

minutes to stop the swelling. A sprain should be covered with a thick layer of cotton. You will also need to put on a bandage, which is fitted tightly. This helps keep swelling down.

Choking

You can tell that someone is choking because they may well be pointing to their throat and won't be able to talk. Slapping a person on the back will help. To move the object that is stuck in the throat, you may need to stand behind the person and place your fist against the stomach, just below the rib cage. Keep on pressing sharply and suddenly. If you are choking, find an adult and point to your throat.

Emergency
- Stay calm.
- Make sure you are not in danger.
- Send for help at once.
- Dial 911, or "0" for operator.
- Know what kind of help you want – police, ambulance or fire brigade.
- Be ready to give the phone number you are using and to say exactly where you are.

- Explain the kind of accident that has happened.
- Stay on the telephone until the person you are talking to hangs up.

Apart from knowing about 911 calls, it's useful to have the telephone number of your doctor, the local hospital and someone who is close to the family. Keep these numbers by the telephone.

Index

Photographic Credits:

Cover and pages 7 (both), 9, 13 (both), 15 (top), 17, 21 and 25 (top): Marie-Helene Bradley; pages 11, 25 (bottom) and 27 (top): David Browne; pages 15 (bottom), 19 (both), 23 (both) and 27 (bottom): CVN Pictures.

PRINTED IN BELGIUM BY
proost
INTERNATIONAL BOOK PRODUCTION